THE FALL OF THE BASTILLE

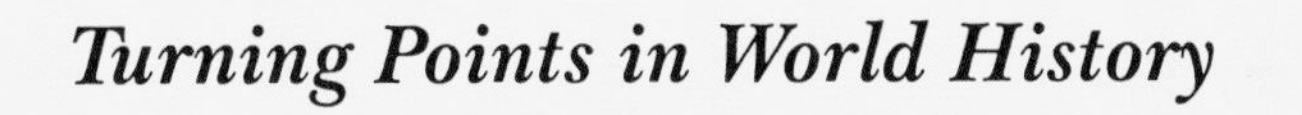

Turning Points in World History

FALL OF THE THE BASTILLE

Kitty C. Benedict

Silver Burdett Press, Inc.

Acknowledgments

The author and editor thank the French Government Tourist Office and Charles Ness for their invaluable help in text and picture research.

Consultants

We thank the following people for reviewing the manuscript and offering their helpful suggestions:

Robert M. Goldberg
Consultant to the Social Studies Department (formerly Department Chair)
Oceanside Middle School
Oceanside, New York

Karen E. Markoe
Professor of History
Maritime College of the State University of New York

Cover: *This painting depicts the storming of the Bastille by a Parisian mob on July 14, 1789. Courtesy of the Bibliothèque Nationale.*

Title Page: *An executioner displays the severed head of King Louis XVI to a revolutionary crowd on January 21, 1793. Courtesy of the French Government Tourist Office.*

Contents Page: *Ordinary household items—like the tobacco box shown here—were often decorated with revolutionary slogans and symbols during the French Revolution. Courtesy of the Mary Evans Picture Library.*

Back Cover: *These French radicals were called* sans-culottes *(without breeches) because they preferred the long pants of workingmen to the shorter knee breeches worn by nobles. Courtesy of the Mary Evans Picture Library.*

Library of Congress Cataloging-in-Publication Data

Benedict, Kitty C.
The Fall of the Bastille / Kitty C. Benedict.
p. cm. -- (Turning points in world history)
Includes bibliographical references and index.
Summary, Describes how the prison known as the Bastille passed from the hands of the government to the hands of the common people, this beginning the French Revolution.
1. Bastille--Juvenile literature. 2. France--History--Revolution, 1789-1799--Juvenile literature. [1. Bastille. 2. France--History--Revolution, 1789-1799.] I. Title. II. Series.
DC167.B38 1991
944.04--dc20 90-26024
CIP
AC

Editorial Coordination by Richard G. Gallin

Created by Media Projects Incorporated

Carter Smith, *Executive Editor*
Charles A. Wills, *Series Editor*
Bernard Schleifer, *Design Consultant*
R. R. Donnelley & Sons Company, *Cartographer*

Manufactured in the United States of America.

ISBN 0-382-24129-0 [lib. bdg.]
10 9 8 7 6 5 4 3 2 1

ISBN 0-382-24135-5 [pbk.]
10 9 8 7 6 5 4 3 2 1

CONTENTS

INTRODUCTION

"To the Bastille!"

It was nearly five o'clock on a hot Tuesday afternoon, July 14, 1789, in Paris. In the courtyard in front of the prison called the Bastille, a grim fourteenth-century fortress, a chaotic struggle had been taking place for seven hours. Gunsmoke still hovered in the air. About eighty people had already been killed and seventy wounded in the fierce fighting. The Bastille had long been a hated symbol of royal power. A person could be imprisoned there by a secret order of the king, with no trial and without a chance to face his accusers.

Shortly after dawn on that day several thousand Parisians had seized 32,000 guns, five cannons, and a mortar at Les Invalides, the old soldiers' hospital. But they had found no gunpowder at the hospital. So the mob, many of them unemployed, had marched through the streets of Paris, shouting "*A la Bastille! A la Bastille*!" ("To the Bastille!"), encouraging others to join them.

A nineteenth-century engraving shows how a mob of Parisians, aided by deserters from the king's army, attacked and captured the Bastille.

About nine hundred people filled the outer courtyard of the Bastille in the working-class district of Saint Antoine. They demanded that the governor of the prison, the Marquis de Launay, hand over 250 barrels of gunpowder stored in the cellars.

Few had planned an attack on the Bastille. Several delegations from the Paris city government had already tried to negotiate with de Launay for the gunpowder. De Launay was asked to give up the Bastille to the new Civil Militia, identifiable by the red and blue ribbons (the colors of Paris) on their hats. Someone spotted a white flag on one of the seventy-five-foot towers of the Bastille. Was the Bastille preparing to surrender?

Suddenly, however, the sound of gunfire split the air. A man fell dead on the ground in front of the prison moat.

This drawing was made by an eyewitness to the fall of the Bastille.

Watching from outside the courtyard, the mob shouted furiously at what it believed was an ambush.

They milled around, angry and confused. No one knew what to do, stunned to find themselves attacking the most potent symbol of royal power in all of France.

Inside the Bastille there was confusion, too. De Launay knew his soldiers weren't eager to fight. Many of them lived in the neighborhood around the Bastille and were friends with the people outside. Only eighty soldiers manned the Bastille, and in spite of the eagerness of the Swiss Guard reinforcements to continue the fight, de Launay began to panic. He had failed to store enough food and water to withstand a siege.

Just then a new group of fighters appeared in the courtyard—French Guards, smartly uniformed, well disciplined, and experienced. They had just deserted from the king's army. They began to set up the cannons taken from the Invalides, aiming them at the Bastille's gate and drawbridges. The crowd shouted "Blow up the bridges!" Suddenly a hand appeared in a slit in the wall near the Bastille's gate. A piece of paper fluttered down.

A plank was thrown across the moat. A man edged over it to take the paper, but fell into the moat. Then an accountant named Maillard stepped bravely across the narrow plank and seized the note. It was a strange message: "Unless you let me surrender, I will blow up the 30,000 pounds of gunpowder, blowing up the Bastille and all the houses around it."

As word of de Launay's threat passed through the crowd, the rumble of their anger arose. It was too late for surrender. "Down with the army!" they shouted. "No surrender!" The French Guards began loading the cannon, but before they could fire, a drawbridge was lowered. Some of the old soldiers inside the Bastille had pushed past de Launay and released the chains holding the drawbridge and gate. The mob surged forward into the main courtyard of the Bastille, attacking anyone and anything in their path. They seized the gunpowder in the prison's cellar. Later that evening they freed the seven dazed prisoners they found.

Incredibly, the Bastille had fallen in an attack by almost unarmed common people. A great rebellion against royal tyranny, the French Revolution, had begun. The storming of the Bastille was marked by the confusion, killing, misunderstanding, and bitter rage that would infect France for the next seven years.

ABOLITION
DE LA
TORTURE

CHAPTER ONE

The Ancien Régime

In France, the winter of 1788–89 was marked by terrible weather. Icy storms froze the rivers, and snow fell for months in the northern provinces. Wine froze in its jugs, and the ground was so hard in places the dead couldn't be buried. Because of the ice on the rivers, mills couldn't turn to grind wheat into flour. In the south of France, frost ruined orchards of apple, orange, and olive trees and devastated vineyards.

Coming on the heels of a drought, in the summer of 1788, the winter was cruel punishment to the peasants eking out a bare existence on the land. Some starved because of the shortage of bread, which was almost all most people had to eat. In a country of 25 million people, about 30,000 were unemployed and homeless, many forced to wander the countryside looking for food.

Louis XVI, who became king of France in 1774. This portrait celebrates the king's 1780 decree forbidding the torture of prisoners.

For workers in France's cities, life was little better. The price of bread rose, while wages fell. Jacques Necker, France's finance minister, imported grain, but fear of famine grew. Tales of hoarding and price-fixing by farmers, merchants, millers, and bakers increased the people's unrest. Mobs raided public granaries, and bread riots broke out in Paris, Caen, Aix, and Rheims.

Yet a few miles outside Paris, at the magnificent royal palace of Versailles, King Louis XVI and his aristocratic courtiers (nobles who lived at the king's court) lived in luxury and splendor. The palace's mirrored galleries and elegant royal apartments had been the scene of balls, concerts, and feasts for a century. From the moment the king got up in the morning, he was waited on by lords and ladies. He dressed in silks, satins, and furs and ate the most delicious meals. The palace was set amid grassy terraces, gardens, lakes, and fountains.

Versailles, Louis XVI's magnificent palace outside Paris.

Louis XVI had been greeted enthusiastically when he came to the throne in 1744. He was a likable man—honest, and deeply religious. He was well educated and owned an extensive library but was very shy. He talked about little besides hunting, his passion. Unfortunately for Louis and for France, affairs of state bored him. He hunted every day. He also loved to tinker with locks in his workshop or build intricate wooden articles.

A large man, Louis seemed fat and awkward. He suffered from indecision when forced to deal with difficult questions. Unsure of himself, he covered up his insecurity with a narrow-minded stubbornness and resistance to compromise, yet he had trouble setting a firm course and sticking to it. He relied heavily on his advisers, who were not always chosen intelligently. His queen, Marie Antoinette, daughter of the empress of Austria, had great influence over him. Her advice was often misguided.

Louis XVI believed firmly in his right to rule France. It was "his" country, granted to him by God Himself. The people of France were "his" people. They might act like unruly children sometimes, but Louis believed they would always respect his divine right to rule.

At first, the people were genuinely fond of the king and his lively queen. One of Louis's first acts as king had been to waive his right to the traditional gift of money from the people to a newly crowned king. He became a devoted family man. He attempted to cut some of the extravagances of the Court. Louis maintained his popularity for some time, even as serious troubles began to arise.

Although the organization of society had changed little for centuries, the world Louis lived in was changing.

Philosophers of the movement called the Enlightenment had focused the light of reason on customs long set by religion and tradition. Writers like Montesquieu, Voltaire, and Rousseau warned of the dangers of tyranny and religious intolerance. They questioned everything in the social and political order, especially the relationship of the people to the state. They believed governments should rule only by the will of the people. They thought all men—they rarely mentioned women—had certain rights and freedoms, such as freedom of speech and the press and the right to a fair trial. They believed in science, in technology, and in progress.

The ancien régime (the old social order), however, was still in place. The people of France were divided into three groups called Estates. The smallest of these, the First Estate, numbering about 100,000 members, was the clergy of the Roman Catholic Church.

The Church had huge wealth and possessions in France. It was well organized and had great influence over local and national government. The highest clergymen—the bishops, archbishops, cardinals, and abbots—were usually men of the nobility. They were rich and educated. The lower ranks of the clergy came from the lower classes of society. They were parish priests and monks. Poor, often uneducated, they lived lives much like the peasants and urban workers they ministered to.

The Church owned about 10 percent of the land in France, collecting taxes from it and its products. The clergy itself paid no taxes at all. The Church controlled schools and hospitals and censored what could be published. It had its own courts of law to administer justice to clergymen and upheld a strict religious system upon which the king's divine right to rule depended. Many French people were religious and respected their local priests, but they distrusted the worldly attitudes and rich living of the upper clergy.

More powerful even than the clergy was the Second Estate—the nobility. Some nobles traced their ancestry back to the earliest days of royalty in France. They had been warriors, proud of their tradition of honor. Many lived on huge estates with beautiful châteaux (manor houses) surrounded by acres of parks, vineyards, forests, and farmland. These dukes, counts, and marquises lived on

This cartoon depicts the First Estate (the clergy) and Second Estate (the nobles) as burdens on the back of the Third Estate (the commoners).

the income from their lands. They alone served as officers in the army and navy, at court, or as the king's ministers and diplomats.

There were only about 400,000 nobles, but they owned 20 percent of the land. Not all members of the Second Estate were wealthy. Some of these aristocrats had lost their lands and wealth, but they clung to the status and privilege given to them by their birth. They tended to be politically conservative and were determined to hold on to their rights and to fight any taxes that might be applied to them.

A significant number in the Second Estate were nobles not by birth but by royal decree. Always needing money, the kings of France had for years sold jobs such as military commissions to wealthy *bourgeois* (middle-class men), giving them titles as well. By 1789, what distinguished a noble from other French people was not wealth but rank as a member of a privileged part of society.

The most important of these privileges was exemption from the main income tax, the *taille* (cut). Nobles themselves collected taxes, fees, and labor from the peasants who lived on their lands. Nobles sat on the regional courts called *parlements*. They had the exclusive hunting rights on their lands, even if it meant riding roughshod through a peasant's crops. They were due respect as feudal lords over the poor peasants and laborers and even the wealthy bourgeois. They could be tried only in their own courts.

A liberal group of nobles—including the Marquis de Lafayette and the Comte de Mirabeau—were influenced by the ideals of the American Revolution and men like Thomas Jefferson and Benjamin Franklin, who had come to France in the late 1770s. Lafayette had served courageously alongside George Washington in the American Revolution, along with other aristocrats such as Mir-

This statue of the Marquis de Lafayette and George Washington was erected in France to honor France's role in helping the American colonies win their independence from Britain.

abeau and the Lameth brothers. These nobles wanted reforms, and they supported the idea of an enlightened king who would rule under a written constitution.

The final order of French society, the Third Estate, included everyone not a member of the nobility or clergy. It numbered about 25 million people, about a million of whom made up the bourgeoisie (middle class). The bourgeoisie included wealthy landowners who owned 20 percent of the land, as well as lawyers, writers, doctors, merchants, and craftsworkers. Traditionally, the term *bourgeoisie* meant city dwellers, but by the eighteenth century the middle class was also found in country towns. Many eagerly copied the manners of the nobility, dressed elegantly, and tried to identify themselves with the aristocracy.

Most of the people of the Third Estate, however, were peasants who worked long hours to earn a bare living from the land. Their lives were difficult, their comforts few. Unlike the clergy and the nobility, the peasants had no tax exemptions. Besides the income tax, the *taille*, they paid tolls to use roads and taxes on salt, tobacco, and wine. They paid fees to use the lord's mill, bakery, and winepress. They also had to provide labor to repair the roads or to transport the military. In addition, they paid a tithe to the Church (10 percent of the value of their produce). In wartime they were chosen by lot to serve in the army. During the 1770s and 1780s, conditions in the country worsened as bad harvests and terrible weather led to an increase in the price of food. Drought followed flood, crops failed, and famines happened frequently.

Another segment of the Third Estate was the men and women who lived in the cities at the bottom of the social and economic scale. They are important to the story of the French Revolution, especially those who lived in Paris, because they provided much of the energy and violence that characterized the revolution. Squeezed between rising prices and lack of work, they were people for whom the risk of rebellion seemed preferable to the misery of their daily lives.

If it had not been for the financial crisis facing France in the 1780s, the French Revolution would not have happened. France, however, was in serious economic trouble as the 1780s drew to a close. France's deficit (the national debt) approached an astonishing 126 million *livres* (one *livre* was worth about $5), partly because of the large amount of money France had contributed to the American Revolution in an effort to fight the country's traditional enemy, Great Britain. By the 1780s, severe reforms were needed in the way money was raised and spent. Too few of the nation's people consumed too much of its wealth.

The king realized the need for financial reform. Most of all, he needed new taxes to save the country from bankruptcy. But the people most able to pay—the First and Second Estates—

were strongly opposed to any taxation on themselves. These people also feared the loss of their traditional privileges because of the growing importance of France's middle class. Some of the clergy and nobility wanted their traditional privileges reinforced, not reduced—a movement called "reinfeudation," or the Feudal Reaction. The Feudal Reaction was opposed by the Third Estate—especially its wealthier members, who believed that they paid more than their share of taxes when compared with the first two estates.

In August 1788, the king reluctantly made an important announcement. Representatives from all three estates—the Estates-General—would meet at Versailles in May 1789 in an attempt to solve the nation's growing problems.

CHAPTER TWO

The Estates-General

The delegates to the Estates-General arrived in Versailles in April 1789 from all over France. The roads were poor, progress was slow, and the heat of an early, dry summer made the journey to Versailles more difficult than ever before.

The delegates brought with them *Cahiers de Doléance* (lists of grievances) from their towns, chiefly pleas for help in a time of economic distress and relief from unequal taxation. They also wanted freedom of the press, regular meetings of the Estates-General, a written constitution, and church reforms. Most of the delegates brought with them strong feelings of loyalty toward the king, for many believed he was sincerely interested in reform. The fact that each of the classes represented at the Estates-General—the clergy, the nobility, and the Third Estate—had hopes for different reforms, and the fact that there might be serious differences within each Estate, were forgotten in the enthusiasm of the moment.

Parisians listen as an author reads from his works at an elegant literary gathering. Educated French men and women in salons like this one discussed the ideas that helped spark the French Revolution.

The Estates-General had not met since 1614. King Louis XVI called them together only because France's economy was in a desperate state. The nation was on the edge of bankruptcy. New sources of revenue were urgently needed.

The king and his ministers had attempted a few changes, such as ending forced labor and establishing judicial reforms. Jacques Necker, the current finance minister, had proposed a general tax on everyone, not just the Third Estate. But when the king tried to get his decrees authorized by the regional *parlements*, which were in the hands of the nobility, the nobles opposed any threat to their privileges or their tax exempt status.

Appeals to the nobles' patriotism and honor proved futile. Although Louis

Jacques Necker, the Swiss-born finance minister who tried to find a solution to France's growing economic troubles. He finally resigned in 1790.

XVI didn't accept any limits to his right to rule, he needed the support of the nobles to raise the money the nation needed. The nobility insisted that only a national assembly had the power to authorize such taxation. The Marquis de Lafayette and others urged the calling of the Estates-General.

During the winter of 1788 and the spring of 1789, the nation set about electing its representatives. The qualifications to be a candidate were based on wealth and property. Tax-paying men of twenty-five or older were allowed to vote for their representatives, but each Estate handled the actual elections differently. For example, all the clergy were eligible for election and were elected directly by other clergy in their district. The noble delegates were also elected directly. In the Third Estate the voters first chose village representatives, who in turn elected the delegates who would attend the Estates-General.

Most of the Third Estate delegates were lawyers. One-fourth were businessmen and civil servants. The rest were soldiers, scholars, and landowners. Only one peasant attended the Estates-General.

Each estate had three hundred delegates voting as a bloc. Each estate had one vote. Thus, the combined votes of the First and Second Estates could easily defeat the Third. When members of the Third Estate realized that they could be outvoted by the nobility and clergy, they were angered. Although at first the Third Estate had eagerly joined with the nobility in calling for the assembly, its delegates now understood that the nobility intended to fight for its special rights and powers. Hoping to gain popular support, the king decreed that the number of delegates from the Third Estate be doubled to 600, though still with only one vote for the entire bloc. The Third Estate delegates, however, arrived at Versailles demanding that each representative have a single vote.

The political energy of the French people had never been so high, fueled by years of growing unrest, social change, and the new Enlightenment ideas about the world and humankind's place in it.

The revolutionary ideas of Jean-Jacques Rousseau were well known. They included the concept that all men had equal rights, that a king ruled not by divine right but by the will of the people, and that special class privileges should be abolished. The Enlightenment had brought a new kind of inquiry into the nature of things, relying on reason and rationality, not on religious teachings. Voltaire wrote about the "natural rights" of men and argued for freedom of speech, religion, and the press. Baron Montesquieu, a lawyer, believed in a monarchy in which a written constitution, or contract, would state the obligations of ruler and ruled.

Political pamphlets began to circulate in the cafés and houses where educated bourgeois French men and women gathered to discuss the new ideas. The recent American Revolution was a vis-

Jean-Jacques Rousseau, one of the Enlightenment thinkers whose writings had great influence on the French Revolution.

ible expression of these ideas. Benjamin Franklin in 1776, and Thomas Jefferson, the U.S. ambassador to France from 1785 to 1789, were important spokesmen in Paris for representative government and individual rights.

One of the most influential writings in France was a pamphlet published in January 1789 titled *What Is the Third Estate?* The author was the Abbot Emmanuel-Joseph de Sieyès, a follower of Voltaire and a radical priest. The pamphlet had a great impact on the debate over the organization of the Estates-General. In it, the abbot answered his own question, "What is the Third Estate?" "The Third Estate is *everything*. What has it been until now? *Nothing*! What does it demand? To become *something*."

With these fiery words, Sieyès stated the case for the Third Estate as the true French nation, the only group able to speak for the country as a whole. "The Third Estate," he wrote, is like "a strong man with one arm in chains. Nothing can work without him. Without the other [the First and Second Estates] everything would work better."

After several frustrating delays (probably because the king's supporters were hoping to postpone the session indefinitely), the Estates-General convened on May 5, 1789. The session opened with great ceremony. A long procession of delegates entered the green and white Grand Hall of Versailles, its walls draped in white silk to mark the occasion. The king, dressed in the finery of a great monarch, made his entrance. The clergy wore rich scarlet robes, while the nobles were in satin and silks with swords and plumed hats. Both contrasted with the Third Estate delegates, who were ordered to wear plain black suits. This careful attention to clothing made the distinction between the estates

The opening of the Estates-General on May 5, 1789. This was one of the few times all three Estates met together.

painfully obvious. By now, the Third Estate knew their interests were not shared by the two other orders.

The next day, the three Estates met in different halls. The delegates of the Third Estate realized that this separation made them even more powerless, so they refused to acknowledge the meetings of the other Estates. For weeks nothing happened but endless, empty debate.

Then, on June 16, nineteen poor parish priests joined the Third Estate. The next day, Sieyès proposed that the Third Estate rename itself a "National Assembly," which could speak for the entire nation. The debate was impassioned, but the proposal passed.

Rumors began to be heard that the king, at the urging of his brother the Comte d'Artois and Queen Marie Antoinette, planned to dissolve the Estates-General and dismiss Necker, but the National Assembly continued to organize itself. An astronomer from Paris, Jean-Sylvain Bailly, was elected as the National Assembly's president.

On the morning of June 20, when the delegates to the National Assembly arrived at their hall, they found the door locked by the king's orders. Standing outside in a pouring rain, about five hundred delegates were told the hall was being renovated for the king's next meeting with the assembly. No one believed this was the real reason. Bailly led the furious delegates to a nearby tennis court, where the session began. Above the shouting, a young lawyer named Jean Joseph Mounier proposed that each member swear "never to leave until a constitution for the kingdom" had been drawn up and accepted. It was called the Tennis Court Oath. At the end of the debate, shouts of "*Vive le Roi!*" ("Long live the king!") filled the air. Even at that dramatic moment, few of the Third Estate (now the National Assembly) had lost faith in the king.

The Estates-General had accomplished little up to this point. The king and the first two estates had held firm to their notions of the *ancien régime*'s rights and privileges, while the Third Estate had begun demanding a constitution, freedom of the press, and an end to unfair taxation. The lowest Estate proclaimed itself the true representatives of the entire nation. The king believed it was an illegitimate gathering but agreed to meet once again with all three Estates on June 23.

In his address, the king let his anger get the better of him. He delivered a humiliating tongue-lashing to the Third Estate. He agreed to ask their consent before for new taxes and to take some limited steps toward freedom of speech. But he denied the commoners' claim to separate status, refused to change any of the privileges of the upper two estates, and prohibited the public from attending any of the sessions of the Estates-General. In his final words—received in angry silence—the king demanded that the National Assembly "Disperse at once and go, each to the chamber intended for your particular order." No shouts of "Long live the king!" were heard.

Nor did the delegates of the Third Estate leave their seats, although the other two estates filed out obediently. Instead, a historic debate, led by Bailly, Mirabeau, and others, took place. In defiance of the king, Mirabeau spoke these memorable words: "We are here by the will of the people and will be removed only by the force of bayonets!"

It was another turning point, a dangerous one, similar to the moment when the signers of the American Declaration of Independence courageously wrote their names at the bottom of that document. The National Assembly, like the Continental Congress in America thirteen years before, was challenging the immense power of the state and the authority of the monarchy itself.

When the king was told of this defiant act, he is said to have shrugged his shoulders: "They want to stay? Well, dammit, let them." Either Louis XVI did not understand what the National Assembly's actions meant, or else he was confident that no rebellion against royal authority could succeed—because at that moment royal troops were arriving in Versailles and Paris from the provinces. There weren't enough troops to take action just yet, but Louis XVI had begun to realize that he couldn't allow the National Assembly to continue on its independent and radical course. The king would have to take action, first against his popular finance minister, Necker, who represented reform, and then against the people themselves.

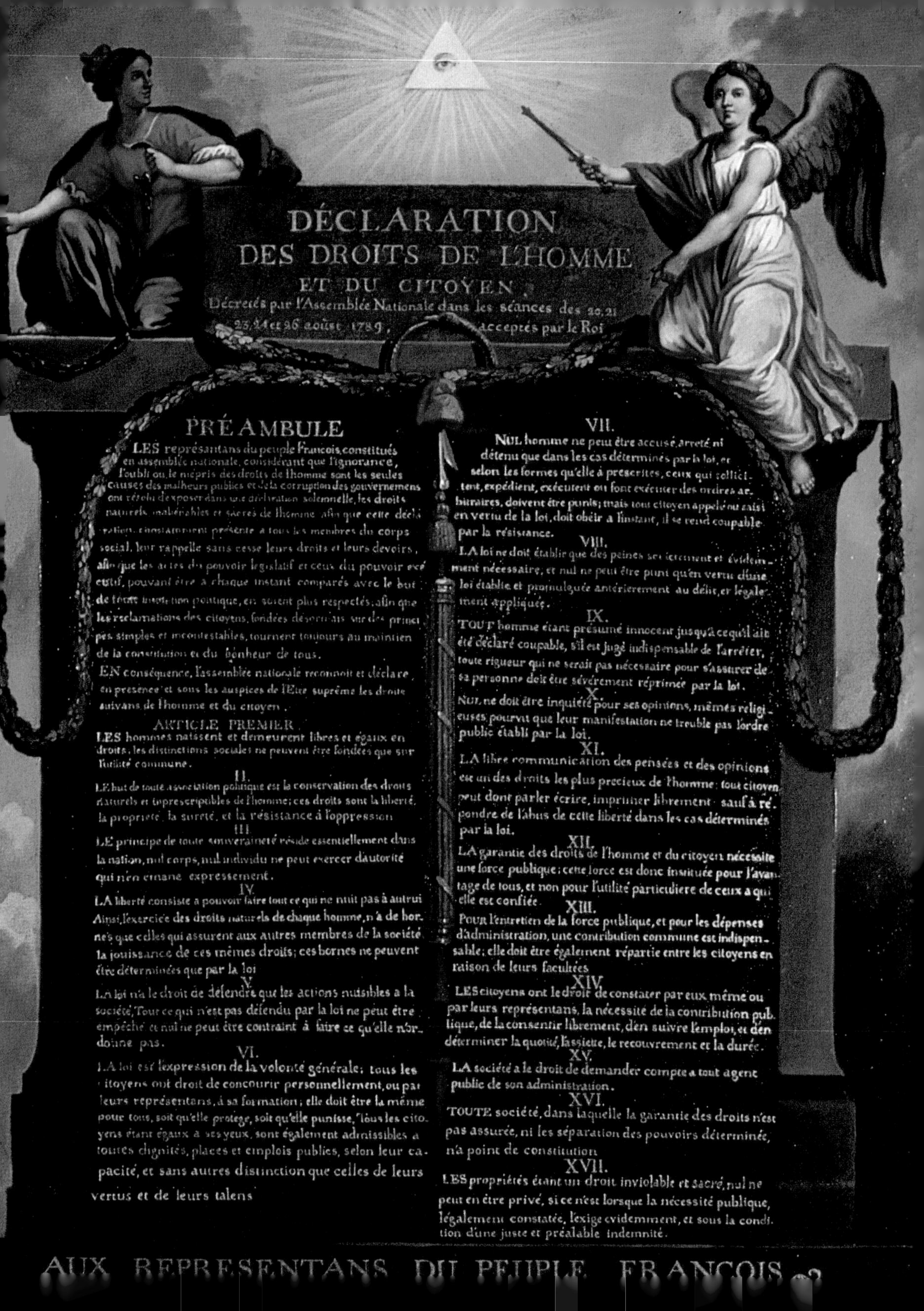

DÉCLARATION DES DROITS DE L'HOMME ET DU CITOYEN,

Décretés par l'Assemblée Nationale dans les séances des 20, 21, 23, 24 et 26 août 1789, acceptés par le Roi

PRÉAMBULE

LES représantans du peuple François, constitués en assemblée nationale, considérant que l'ignorance, l'oubli ou le mépris des droits de l'homme sont les seules causes des malheurs publics et de la corruption des gouvernemens ont résolu d'exposer dans une déclaration solemnelle, les droits naturels inaliénables et sacrés de l'homme afin que cette déclaration constamment présente à tous les membres du corps social, leur rappelle sans cesse leurs droits et leurs devoirs, afin que les actes du pouvoir legislatif et ceux du pouvoir exécutif, pouvant être à chaque instant comparés avec le but de toute institution politique, en soient plus respectés; afin que les reclamations des citoyens, fondées désormais sur des principes simples et incontestables, tournent toujours au maintien de la constitution et du bonheur de tous.

EN conséquence, l'assemblée nationale reconnoit et déclare en presence et sous les auspices de l'Etre suprême les droits suivans de l'homme et du citoyen.

ARTICLE PREMIER.

LES hommes naissent et demeurent libres et égaux en droits, les distinctions sociales ne peuvent être fondées que sur l'utilité commune.

II.

LE but de toute association politique est la conservation des droits naturels et imprescriptibles de l'homme; ces droits sont la liberté, la propriété, la sureté, et la résistance à l'oppression.

III.

LE principe de toute souveraineté réside essentiellement dans la nation, nul corps, nul individu ne peut exercer d'autorité qui n'en émane expressement.

IV.

LA liberté consiste à pouvoir faire tout ce qui ne nuit pas à autrui. Ainsi, l'exercice des droits naturels de chaque homme, n'a de bornes que celles qui assurent aux autres membres de la société la jouissance de ces mêmes droits; ces bornes ne peuvent être déterminées que par la loi.

V.

LA loi n'a le droit de défendre que les actions nuisibles à la société, Tout ce qui n'est pas défendu par la loi ne peut être empêché et nul ne peut être contraint à faire ce qu'elle n'ordonne pas.

VI.

LA loi est l'expression de la volonté générale; tous les citoyens ont droit de concourir personnellement, ou par leurs représentans, à sa formation; elle doit être la même pour tous, soit qu'elle protege, soit qu'elle punisse, Tous les citoyens étant égaux à ses yeux, sont également admissibles à toutes dignités, places et emplois publics, selon leur capacité, et sans autres distinction que celles de leurs vertus et de leurs talens.

VII.

NUL homme ne peut être accusé, arreté ni détenu que dans les cas déterminés par la loi, et selon les formes qu'elle à prescrites, ceux qui sollicitent, expédient, exécutent ou font exécuter des ordres arbitraires, doivent être punis; mais tout citoyen appelé ou saisi en vertu de la loi, doit obéir à l'instant, il se rend coupable par la résistance.

VIII.

LA loi ne doit établir que des peines strictement et évidemment nécessaire, et nul ne peut être puni qu'en vertu d'une loi établie et promulguée antérieurement au délit, et légalement appliquée.

IX.

TOUT homme étant présumé innocent jusqu'à ce qu'il ait été déclaré coupable, s'il est jugé indispensable de l'arrêter, toute rigueur qui ne serait pas nécessaire pour s'assurer de sa personne doit être sévérement réprimée par la loi.

X.

NUL ne doit être inquiété pour ses opinions, mêmes religieuses pourvu que leur manifestation ne trouble pas l'ordre public établi par la loi.

XI.

LA libre communication des pensées et des opinions est un des droits les plus precieux de l'homme: tout citoyen peut dont parler écrire, imprimer librement sauf à répondre de l'abus de cette liberté dans les cas déterminés par la loi.

XII.

LA garantie des droits de l'homme et du citoyen nécessite une force publique: cette force est donc instituée pour l'avantage de tous, et non pour l'utilité particuliere de ceux à qui elle est confiée.

XIII.

POUR l'entretien de la force publique, et pour les dépenses d'administration, une contribution commune est indispensable; elle doit être également répartie entre les citoyens en raison de leurs facultés.

XIV.

LES citoyens ont le droit de constater par eux même ou par leurs représentans, la nécessité de la contribution publique, de la consentir librement, d'en suivre l'emploi, et d'en déterminer la quotité, l'assiette, le recouvrement et la durée.

XV.

LA société a le droit de demander compte à tout agent public de son administration.

XVI.

TOUTE société, dans laquelle la garantie des droits n'est pas assurée, ni les séparation des pouvoirs déterminée, n'a point de constitution.

XVII.

LES propriétés étant un droit inviolable et sacré, nul ne peut en être privé, si ce n'est lorsque la nécessité publique, légalement constatée, l'exige evidemment, et sous la condition d'une juste et préalable indemnité.

AUX REPRESENTANS DU PEUPLE FRANCOIS

CHAPTER THREE

Year of Riot and Revolution

July 14, 1789, was a hot day in Paris. The sky was overcast, with large gray clouds threatening rain. As usual, King Louis XVI spent the day hunting in the woods around Versailles. That night, he wrote a one-word entry in his hunting journal: "Rien" (nothing).

Twelve miles away in Paris, the streets were filling with crowds. The news that the king had fired Finance Minister Necker had led to wild rumors. An economic collapse was feared. The Parisians were worried by reports that royal troops were camped in the Champ de Mars, the parade ground of the military academy. Many people were out of work and hungry because of the rising price of bread. Above all, they feared that the king would dissolve the National Assembly and order his troops to attack the city.

An ornamental print of the Declaration of the Rights of Man and Citizen adopted by the National Assembly in August 1789.

On Sunday, July 12, crowds had gathered in the Palais Royal to talk, drink, and hear the latest news. The Palais Royal was a popular place of entertainment. It was a hotbed of political activity where speakers addressed the strolling crowds. That afternoon, a young unemployed lawyer named Camille Desmoulins whipped the crowd into a near frenzy. Standing on a table outside the Café du Foy, he spoke angrily of the dangers threatening the city from the king, his army, and the upper classes. He told his listeners to prepare for battle, shouting, "To arms! To arms! The king and his battalions are preparing to murder the citizens of Paris!"

From that moment until the evening of July 14, Paris was aflame with looting, rioting, and arson. A half-million people lived in the city's narrow, crowded streets, most of them in miserable conditions. Especially badly off were the poor laborers, shopkeepers, and craftsmen who lived in districts like

Parisian lawyer Camille Desmoulins urges the crowd at the Palais Royal to march on the Bastille.

A French cartoon celebrates the destruction of the Bastille.

Saint Antoine and Saint Marcel, not far from the old royal prison—the Bastille.

On the morning of July 14, fifteen cannons had been set up on the walls of the Bastille. It looked as if the troops inside planned to fire on the Saint Antoine district. Once a fortress, the Bastille had been built in 1370 to guard one of Paris's city gates. Its walls were 100 feet high and 8 feet thick. It was little used as a prison in 1789, but its grim bulk had long stood as a symbol of royal power.

The Bastille was a special kind of prison. Ordinary criminals weren't sent there; it was reserved for those who committed crimes against the state—spies, forgers, religious heretics, and antigovernment writers.

Frightened and angry Parisians had seized over thirty thousand guns, but they had no gunpowder. They knew that the Bastille held a supply of gunpowder, so an angry mob had headed for the old prison. By midmorning, hundreds of people had gathered in the courtyard in front of the prison to demand gunpowder. A delegation from the Paris city government arrived to negotiate with the prison's commander, de Launay. Eager to calm the mob, he took the delegation on a tour of the Bastille.

De Launay showed them that the prison's cannons weren't loaded but refused to hand over the powder. As the day wore on, the crowd outside the Bastille grew more excited.

Despite many eyewitness accounts, it isn't known who fired the first shot at the Bastille. In the midst of the confusion and the shouting, shots exploded in the outer courtyard at noon. By 2:00 P.M., eighty people lay dead. Seventy more had been wounded. De Launay offered to surrender, but it was too late for negotiations. The battle continued until the evening. The mob, now joined by the city militia and French Guards, stormed the prison. The handful of prisoners were released, the ammunition was seized, and the Bastille's defenders were taken prisoner. The victorious attackers paraded through the streets of Paris, taking de Launay with them. On the way to the city hall, someone stabbed de Launay, who was then beheaded by one of the rioters. His head, stuck on a pitchfork, was displayed at the front of the procession. It was an ominous beginning to the French Revolution.

At Versailles, the rioting seemed just another in the series of disturbances common in the unruly city of Paris. When a courtier entered the king's bedroom to tell him of the Bastille's fall, the king asked, "Is it a revolt?" "No, sire," he replied, "it is a *revolution*!"

A few days later, the king himself came to Paris to declare his peaceful intentions to the rebellious citizens. He appeared before the people wearing the revolutionary colors: red, white, and blue. He confirmed the appointment of Bailly as mayor of the new city government. Lafayette was named commander of the National Guard, the militia formed by the middle class to protect property and keep order. But the king's actions did little to stem the rising tide of fear and anger that had taken hold in the countryside as well as in Paris.

Nothing had changed for the peasants. Angry and impatient, they were easily worried by rumors. Some said the nobility was about to attack the peasants by hiring mobs of bandits to rob them and destroy their crops.

During July and August, a period called the Great Fear, the peasants rose up in revolt. They killed nobles and burned their houses, destroyed tax records in town halls, and forced other nobles to give up their ancient privileges. Many of these aristocrats fled across the borders. Local governments broke down as officials were tossed out of office and replaced by members of the bourgeoisie.

Frightened by the unrest in the countryside, the National Assembly met on August 4 to debate a proposal to abolish feudal privileges. It was overwhelmingly approved. The Church tithe was ended, feudal taxes were done away with, and a general income tax was approved. Reform in the courts and the Church was begun. When these measures were written into law, worried bourgeoisie backtracked somewhat and demanded that landowners be paid for their loss of income. Nevertheless, the August 4, 1789,

Peasants loot a noble's home in the wave of unrest that followed the fall of the Bastille.

decrees were an important step in freeing France from its feudal state. From then on, the Revolution was out of the hands of the nobles, whose resistance to taxes and reform had first brought on the struggle.

The most significant act of the National Assembly that summer was the Declaration of the Rights of Man and Citizen. The document, drafted by Lafayette, was adopted on August 26. The Declaration reflected the ideas of the Enlightenment and the writings of Voltaire, Rousseau, and the Englishman John Locke. The Declaration began by stating, "Nature has made all men free and equal," that "the government exists for the benefit of those who are governed, not of those who govern." The Declaration said that a free press is "the strongest supporter of freedom," and that government must "guarantee . . . rights such as personal liberty, property, security, the protection of honor and

The revolutionary mob marches from Paris to Versailles in October 1789 in this nineteenth-century engraving.

life, free expression of thought and resistance to oppression." These rights were proclaimed for all men everywhere, although not for women.

Five weeks later, the National Assembly took another important step by passing an act taking away the king's right to absolute power. The government was divided into three parts: the executive (the king and his ministers), the legislative, and the judicial. The king had to accept laws passed by the assembly, although he could suspend them for four years. He was forbidden from making laws.

At this point the king saw that his power was being cut away. Once more he called royal troops to Versailles. He announced his intention to study the assembly's proposal, but in reality he was stalling for time.

On October 1, the king and queen held a lavish banquet to honor the officers of a regiment that had just arrived at Versailles. During the evening the officers toasted the king, yelled insulting jokes about the revolution, and finally trampled revolutionary tricolor ribbons underfoot. News of this orgy of banqueting in the midst of grave food shortages quickly reached Paris. On the cold, rainy day of October 5, Paris again exploded into riots. This time a mob of poor women, angered at the lack of bread, took to the streets.

After a four-hour march, during which the women were joined by many of the "conquerors of the Bastille," the crowd arrived at Versailles. Six of the marchers were chosen to present their grievances to the king. Louis received them politely and promised he would send grain to Paris. But when the National Assembly sent a delegation to the king to demand he approve the Declaration of the Rights of Man and the new organization of the government, Louis hesitated. Finally, with tears of rage in his eyes, he promised he would sign.

During the night, as rain-soaked crowds roamed the streets of Versailles, a small group of people found an unlocked door to the palace. They burst in hoping to seize the queen. Instead they murdered two of the king's bodyguards with pikes (long sharpened poles)—another symbol in this revolution of many symbols.

The mob was now determined to bring the king himself to Paris. The National Guard had forced its commander, Lafayette, to lead them to Versailles to protect the protesting women. Unwilling to jeopardize his popularity with both the king and the people, Lafayette hesitated. However, determined to protect the king, he marched to Versailles with 15,000 guards.

On the evening of October 6, the king, the queen, and their son were taken to Paris. The heads of the murdered bodyguards, stuck on the pikes, led the procession. It was another ominous sign of the violent direction the Revolution would take.

Soon after, the National Assembly also moved to Paris. The influence of the city and its people was important, as the Parisians were more radical and politically aware than the rest of the French. The most radical of all were the so-called *sans-culottes* (without breeches), workmen who wore long pants instead of the short breeches worn by the aristocracy and wealthy bourgeoisie.

Paris was also home to publishing and journalism, which were so important in spreading the ideas of the Revolution. Because of the new freedom of the press, scores of books, pamphlets, and newspapers were rushed into print. Every political point of view was published. Some journals were satirical and scandalous; some were not always based on fact. One of the most popular, *L'Ami du Peuple* ("The Friend of the People"), was published by the violent revolutionary Jean-Paul Marat. It often contained more propaganda than truth, written to encourage the radical actions he proposed. Marat was one of the first to call for the king's death.

In Paris, the assembly became more radical when three hundred royalist members, dissatisfied with the turn the Revolution was taking, resigned and fled abroad. The remaining delegates began to meet in the Manège (riding school) near the Tuileries Palace, where the royal family lived as virtual prisoners. The National Assembly began to split into factions, each with different political aims. The Centrist party of Lafayette and Mirabeau sat in the center of the hall. They wanted a constitutional monarchy, in which the king's power would be limited by a constitution and balanced by a legislature. To the right of the president's chair sat the remaining royalists, the conservatives. On the left sat the most extreme revolutionary groups, the Jacobins, Girondins, and Cordeliers. (These seating arrangements—left, center, and right—have continued as political labels into our own era.) These "parties" originated as political debating clubs, taking their names from the places where they met. Maximilien Robespierre was one of the leaders of the Jacobins. Georges Jacques Danton, a lawyer and a powerful orator, became president of the Cordeliers, whose members were not as well off as the middle-class Jacobins.

As 1789 ended, France's economic problems remained unsolved. A solution was proposed by Abbot Charles de Talleyrand, an aristocratic clergyman, and agreed to by the Assembly in November. According to Talleyrand's plan, all church-owned lands, amounting in value to about 2 million livres (about $10 billion), were confiscated by the government and "put at the disposal of the nation." Bank notes called *assignats*, which could be exchanged for church lands, were issued for sale. Eventually these *assignats* became legal currency. The scheme never really reduced France's national debt. The financial crisis continued.

Many of the seeds of future violence were planted at this time. The assembly was now made up largely of middle-class men of property. When the electoral rules were drawn up, only males twenty-five years or older who could pay taxes worth three days' work were eligible to vote. (This doesn't seem democratic by today's standards, but it was a major step forward for Europe at that time.) Those who owned property could hold office. While about 4 million French people could vote under the new rules, five times that number could not—including women, slaves, free blacks, and, at first, Jews and other non-Catholics. The split between the middle classes and the lower classes widened, and the *sans-culottes*' dissatisfaction with the Revolution increased.

Nevertheless, in 1790 the Assembly continued work on the constitution. On the surface, 1790 was peaceful. But the king and queen had begun to play a double game, publicly supporting the revolution while privately scheming with allies and sympathizers in France and abroad.

All divisions in France were forgotten, however, in the celebrations marking the first anniversary of the fall of the Bastille. The Fête de la Fédération (Festival of Federation) took place on July 14, 1790, on the Champ de Mars parade ground. The Parisians worked fever-

The Marquis de Lafayette swears allegiance to the law and people of France at the July 1790 Festival of the Federation. The celebration marked the first anniversary of the fall of the Bastille.

ishly to prepare the site, building a huge amphitheater, an altar to the nation, and an enormous triumphal arch.

On the great day, the National Guard gathered in military splendor to swear allegiance to the nation, the law, and the crown. The king and queen, dressed in red, white, and blue, reviewed the troops. Banners from all over France were paraded. As organ music swelled over the 300,000 people in attendance, Talleyrand said a High Mass. Lafayette swore to uphold the law and the constitution, and to be bound by the ties of fraternity (brotherhood) to all the people of France. The king swore to "maintain and see the laws upheld." The guns of the National Guard fired in celebration. It seemed as if the revolution had been accomplished. All France rejoiced in a grand display of unity, brotherhood, and liberty.

CHAPTER FOUR

The Revolution Is Radicalized

In spite of the national unity expressed by the Fête de la Fédération, the divisions within French society were deepening. Also in July 1790, the National Assembly passed an act, called the Civil Constitution of the Clergy, heightening these divisions. The government took control of the Catholic Church. Parish priests and bishops were to be elected by the people. The state paid the clergy's wages. The king reluctantly signed the act but he was angered by this attack on France's traditional faith. In the fall of 1790, as the first confiscated church lands were sold, the National Assembly passed the Oath of Allegiance. This act required all the clergy to swear an oath of loyalty to the revolution.

Many French people were opposed to the Revolution's attack on the Church. Violent protests sprang up in some regions. When the Pope denounced the National Assembly's decrees, the split between religious and anti-clerical (anti-clergy) groups grew worse. Many people who had once been sympathetic to the ideals of the revolution joined nonjuring priests in forming counter-revolutionary groups. (A nonjuring priest was one who refused to sign the loyalty oath.) More than half the priests in France refused to sign.

Maximilien Robespierre, the "incorruptible" leader of the radical Jacobin political party.

Many nobles continued to leave France. Called émigrés, many joined an army formed by the Comte d'Artois and the Comte de Provence, the king's brothers. Some émigrés sought support from foreign rulers for an invasion of France to restore the power of the monarchy. European royalty nervously watched the events in France. If revolution could happen there, where would it strike next? This uneasiness was fueled by letters written by the king and Marie Antoinette, especially to Marie's brother, Leopold, emperor of the Holy Roman Empire in central Europe.

The royal family's attempt to escape ends at Varennes.

Louis was stung into action after the Assembly passed the Civil Constitution of the Clergy. He agreed to attempt an escape from the Tuileries Palace. On the night of June 20, 1791, the king and queen and their two children disguised themselves as servants. A coach took them to the outskirts of Paris, where they switched to another coach. The plan was to head northeast to Montmédy, near the Luxembourg border. There, royalists would protect the king and rally support for the restoration of the monarchy.

Unfortunately for the royal family, their huge carriage made slow progress. A loyal cavalry unit waited to escort the carriage, but after it failed to arrive they rode off, thinking the plan had been canceled. The villagers in the next town became suspicious when the elegant coach from Paris passed through. The village postmaster, Jean Baptiste Drouet, thought he recognized the queen among the coach's passengers. Later that afternoon, Drouet heard that the royal family had escaped from Paris. Leaping on his horse, he rode to the town of Varennes, where the royal coach had stopped. Drouet told the people of Varennes about his suspicions. A judge was called to look at the travelers. When the judge instinctively dropped to one knee in recognition of the king, Louis confessed, "Yes, I am your king." The royal family was handed over to the National Guard and immediately taken back to Paris.

To the revolution's leaders, the escape attempt made it clear that the king wasn't trustworthy. Foolishly, the king had left papers behind denouncing the Revolution's reforms. Fears of foreign invasion and aristocratic plots flared up.

Meanwhile, the Cordeliers political club called for an end to the monarchy and the creation of a republic—a nation based on representative government with no monarch. The Cordeliers' leaders included Georges Danton and the bloodthirsty Jean-Paul Marat. Most Cordeliers were *sans-culottes*—laborers, craftsmen, and small businessmen. In fiery words, Marat demanded the king's removal.

The National Assembly had nearly finished work on the 1791 constitution. When the National Assembly voted to restore the king's limited powers if he accepted the constitution, the Cordeliers began circulating petitions for the trial of the king. Refused a hearing by the National Assembly, they decided to

Georges Jacques Danton, president of the Cordeliers Club, speaks before the Assembly.

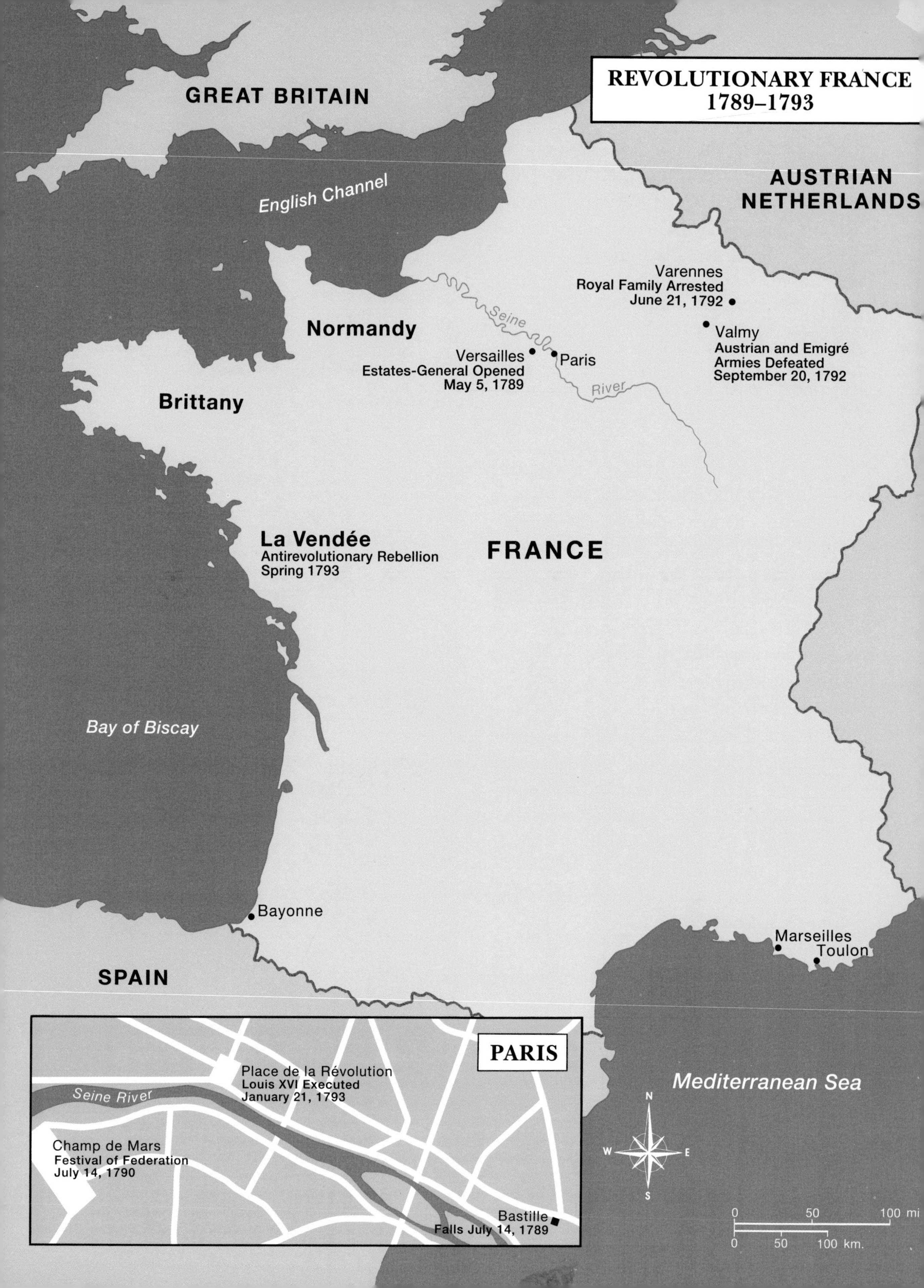
REVOLUTIONARY FRANCE
1789–1793
GREAT BRITAIN
English Channel
AUSTRIAN
NETHERLANDS
Varennes
Royal Family Arrested
June 21, 1792
Seine
Normandy
Valmy
Austrian and Emigré
Armies Defeated
September 20, 1792
Versailles
Estates-General Opened
May 5, 1789
Paris
River
Brittany
La Vendée
Antirevolutionary Rebellion
Spring 1793
FRANCE
Bay of Biscay
Bayonne
Marseilles
Toulon
SPAIN
PARIS
Place de la Révolution
Louis XVI Executed
January 21, 1793
Seine River
Champ de Mars
Festival of Federation
July 14, 1790
Bastille
Falls July 14, 1789
Mediterranean Sea
N
W
E
S
0
50
100 mi
0
50
100 km.

stage a huge rally at the Champ de Mars at which people could sign the petitions.

Some members of the Jacobin Club, including Maximilien Robespierre, supported the Cordeliers. Other leaders, like the more conservative Lafayette, supported the middle class, who wanted to maintain law and order. The unity of the revolution had splintered. The basic split was between those who wanted to preserve the monarchy in a limited way and those who wanted to remove the king. The second group—the republicans—wanted a more democratic government in which every man, regardless of wealth and property, would have civil and political rights. There were even a few who tried to win equal political rights for women.

During the July 17 rally at the Champ de Mars, two men were seized and accused of being counterrevolutionary spies. Before they could be taken to jail, the crowd hanged them on the spot. Alarmed, the National Assembly ordered Lafayette and the National Guard to put down the rioting. Martial law was declared, and by the end of the day the Guard had killed at least fifty of the demonstrators. The leaders of the Cordeliers went into hiding: Danton fled to England, and Marat hid in the sewers of Paris. Lafayette's popularity with the people disappeared overnight.

On September 3, 1791, the new constitution passed into law. Louis XVI declared his allegiance to the constitution a few days later, although it greatly limited his power. The constitution protected wealth and property rights, which were important to the bourgeoisie, while guaranteeing free speech and ending all privileges of the clergy and nobility.

To some, the passage of the constitution seemed to mark the end of the revolution. But there was also great disappointment. The lower classes felt the Constitution of 1791 betrayed the spirit of 1789 and the Declaration of the Rights of Man. The split between the middle class and the "people"—the *sans-culottes* in the city and the angry peasants in the country—was deep and growing. To these people, it seemed that the *ancien régime* had merely been replaced by a new aristocracy based on money.

An election was needed to choose representatives to the new Legislative Assembly. Robespierre pushed through a proposal forbidding the reelection of any former delegates. "The revolution is not over," he said. A new group of delegates were elected, many of them dissatisfied with the constitution.

The Legislative Assembly included the conservatives on the right, led by Lafayette, who still wanted a limited monarchy. On the left were the Jacobins and Girondins, known as "the Mountain," because they sat on raised seats. They represented the *sans-culottes* and other radical groups. The majority in the Center were moderates.

The most powerful faction in the Legislative Assembly was a group of deputies from the Gironde area. They believed in Rousseau's ideals of personal liberty. But they were inexperienced in the practical dealings of government.

Another rising star in the Legislative Assembly was the Jacobin leader Robespierre. He was a humorless, uncompromising man who considered himself the "defender of liberty" and the Revolution. Nicknamed "the Incorruptible," Robespierre was a master politician.

France continued to face serious problems, including inflation, unemployment, and falling wages. Despite good harvests, there were shortages of food as merchants held back produce to keep prices high. The Girondins were not eager to confront these problems.

Inexperienced, or because they had no solutions, the Girondins chose not to face France's tough economic and social problems. Instead, they attacked "enemies of the revolution" by passing a decree calling for the execution of any émigré noble who refused to return from exile. Also, they used the threat of foreign invasion to rally the people and distract them from the problems at home.

The Girondins decided to call for a war on the émigrés and their supporters in Austria, Prussia, and Belgium. They wanted a "crusade" to take the principles of liberty and equality to the rest of Europe. On April 20, 1792, the Legislative Assembly declared war on Austria, which had formed an anti-French alliance with several other nations.

The king supported the war but for a very different reason: He hoped an Austrian victory would restore him to power. Lafayette, too, was eager to fight. He was ambitious for national leadership and wanted the glory a French victory would bring. Radicals like Marat hoped the war would completely destroy the last traces of monarchy in France.

At first, the French Army was badly defeated by the Austrians. Many of the army's best officers had fled abroad, and the soldiers were badly trained and undisciplined. Shocked, the Girondins tried to blame the king and other "enemies of the revolution." The king fired the Girondin minister and vetoed the decrees against the émigrés and the nonjuring priests.

But the *sans-culottes* were in an unruly mood. In Paris, they demonstrated in the streets in favor of limits on the price of food. Control of the revolution was shifting from the Legislative Assembly into the hands of angry, violent mobs. In the countryside, food riots were common. Fears of invasion grew. When the king vetoed the Legislative Assembly's call for 20,000 volunteer soldiers to defend Paris, the *sans-culottes* of the city and the peasants of the provinces took action on their own.

On June 20, a mob of about eight thousand Parisians burst into the Legislative Assembly's morning session. They were armed with pikes, clubs, and guns—any weapon they could get their hands on. They moved on to the Tuileries, where they confronted the king, screaming their opposition to his vetoes. The mob forced the king to put on a red cap, another symbol of the Revolution. The king remained calm in the face of

Wearing "liberty caps" and carrying signs denouncing the king's veto of revolutionary legislation, a mob confronts Louis XVI in the Tuileries Palace in June 1792.

A later engraving depicts the violence of the "September Massacres" in Paris in September 1792.

these insults. Eventually the mob drifted away. Not much had been accomplished, but the idea of a violent encounter with the king was no longer unthinkable.

Austria now threatened to invade France. The National Guardsmen in the provinces, the *Féderés*, marched to Paris, arriving in the hot July of 1792. The Guard was no longer interested in maintaining order. They wanted a republic and they were willing to take violent action against anyone who opposed them. Paris was soon in the hands of the *Féderés* and their radical supporters. They threatened to seize the Tuileries unless the Legislative Assembly removed the king from the government of France. Jean-Paul Marat and other radical journalists began circulating rumors in Paris that jailed nonjuring priests and royalists were plotting to overthrow the revolution. The radicals spoke of "people's justice." They demanded death for "traitors and enemies of the revolution!"

Before the Legislative Assembly could act, the radicals made good on their threat. On August 10, mobs attacked the palace, massacring the royal bodyguards. For the revolutionaries, the attack on the Tuileries ranked with the fall of the Bastille as a day of triumph. Fearing more violence, the Legislative Assembly quickly voted to remove Louis XVI from power. The king and his family were arrested and imprisoned. The Legislative Assembly also decided to hold elections for a new legislative body—the National Convention. In the meantime, an executive council of six ministers was appointed to govern France. Five ministers were Girondins. The sixth, the Minister of Justice, was George Jacques Danton, founder of the Cordeliers Club. A radical, popular with the common people of Paris, Danton was willing to sacrifice anything for the revolution.

Meanwhile, the war with Austria continued to go badly. By the end of August, Austrian, Prussian, and émigré armies led by the Duke of Brunswick had crossed France's border with the Netherlands. At Longwy, the invaders defeated the still-disorganized French army. Paris was only a few days' march away, and the enemy seemed headed straight for it.

On September 2, Danton addressed the Legislative Assembly, appealing to all citizens to defend Paris. As he spoke, church bells tolled. "It is time, gentlemen," Danton said, "for the Assembly to become a true council of war. The bells are a signal to charge against the enemies of our country. . . . To defeat them we need boldness, and again boldness, and always boldness, and France will then be saved!" Soon, thousands of Parisians armed themselves and marched toward the Prussian and Austrian armies at the town of Valmy, just one hundred miles from Paris.

Danton may have meant to rally the people against the invading armies. But there was too much pent-up anger in Paris for it to end there. The *sans-culottes* and other radicals lashed out at revolutionary enemies they saw at home. For

French troops halt the invading Austrian and émigré army at the Battle of Valmy on September 20, 1792.

five days, bloodthirsty mobs attacked the jails of Paris and butchered the priests, nobles, and royalists imprisoned there. A kind of madness took over. Many innocent victims died during these horrible days, called the September Massacres, which left 1,200 dead in Paris. The madness spread to the provinces. Hundreds more died in cities like Rheims, Lyons, and Marseilles. Leaders like Robespierre, Danton, and the Girondins might have tried to stop the slaughter, but they didn't.

At the Battle of Valmy on September 20, 1792, the French army at last halted the foreign advance. For the moment, at least, the French Revolution was saved.

On September 21, just one day after the victory at Valmy, the new National Convention met publicly for the first

time and decreed "Royalty is abolished in France." Thus, on September 21, 1792, the monarchy ended. The next day the Convention declared France a republic. In November, the Convention announced that France was willing to help any other nation that wanted to overthrow its royal rulers and establish a government based on the principles of Liberté, Egalité, and Fraternité—liberty, equality, and fraternity. The Revolution was to be exported.

The French Revolution had begun as an aristocratic revolt against taxation by the king. It developed into a middle-class movement for individual liberty and freedom from aristocratic privilege. Now the Revolution was in the hands of the most radical groups, moving ever more into chaos and violence.

EGALITÉ

CHAPTER FIVE

The Terror

After the king's arrest, the Convention passed reforms reflecting the growing influence of the *sans-culottes. All* males over the age of twenty-five were given the right to vote. Nonjuring priests were to be expelled from the country. All remaining feudal dues owed to landlords were ended, and the king's powers were suspended.

There were now two main groups in the revolutionary government. On the left was "the Mountain"—the Jacobins. They drew support from the Paris Commune (the city's revolutionary government) and the *sans-culottes*. On the right were the Girondins, representing, for the most part, the people of the provinces, who tended to be conservative. Those in the middle were called "the Plain."

The most extreme of the Jacobins were the *enragés* ("madmen"), who favored tight controls on wages and prices. The Girondins—most of them—were disgusted by the violence of September. They were also opposed to any restrictions on the free market.

As 1792 ended, one question was on everyone's mind: What should be done with the king? The radicals wanted him tried as an "enemy of the state." In November 1792, the debate over the king's fate began in the Convention. One fanatical Jacobin, twenty-year-old Louis de Saint-Just, argued that Louis XVI should be not only tried but executed as well. The Girondins attempted to stall, but the king's secret letters to foreign allies were discovered. A stormy trial began in the Convention.

On January 14, 1793, the Convention began voting on the king's fate. The ballots were cast by individual roll call as the public watched. The verdict was announced on January 20: Louis Capet, king of the French, was found guilty of

In this antirevolutionary cartoon, the radical Philippe Egalité (formerly the Duc d'Orléans) displays the severed head of his cousin, King Louis XVI.

The trial of King Louis XVI. The king is shown at right.

conspiracy. Out of the Convention's 721 members, all but 38 had voted against the king. Then by a majority of one vote—361 to 360—he was condemmed to death. Even the king's cousin the Duc d'Orléans—now a radical who called himself Philippe Egalité—had voted for execution.

On January 21, Louis XVI was taken to the guillotine set up in the Place de la Revolution—formerly called the Place de Louis XVI. The square was crowded with Parisians, silent at the sight of the condemned monarch. A cold rain fell as Louis walked alone up the steps to the platform. Drums beat out a steady roll, falling silent only as the king began to speak: "My people, I die innocent. . . ." But the drums rolled again, drowning out his voice. The king was tied to the machine; the blade fell downward, severing his head. The executioner grasped the head of Louis XVI and held it up for the crowd to see. A cry went up: "The king is dead; Long live the Republic!"

The king's execution sent a wave of shock and outrage throughout the

The king prepares to go to the guillotine.

courts of Europe—and in parts of France. In the spring of 1793, rebels in Brittany and the Vendée rose up in rebellion. In several battles, bands of farmers and royalists defeated the National Guard and took control of towns and cities. Eventually, revolutionary forces put down these uprisings with great brutality and loss of life. And the conflicts with other nations continued. In February 1793, France had declared war on Britain and Spain. In April, the war in Belgium began to go badly for France. This put the Girondins, still in power, under strong attack from the "Mountain," led by Marat, Danton, and Robespierre.

Marat accused the Girondins of betraying the Revolution. Danton called for the establishment of a "Revolutionary Tribunal" to "try all counterrevolutionary acts, and . . . all plots hostile to the liberty, equality, and sovereign rights of the people." The Tribunal was soon dominated by the Mountain and the *sans-culottes.* Danton said, "Let us embody terror so as to prevent the people from doing so." The Tribunal consisted

Charlotte Corday, who assassinated Jean-Paul Marat in July 1793.

of five judges and twelve jurors. They set out to find and punish priests, nobles, and hoarders of food and money. In every part of the country, "watch committees" were set up to "discover and prevent evil."

On April 6, 1793, the leftist factions created the Committee of Public Safety to take over the war effort. Declaring a state of emergency, the committee—which met in secret—declared it would also run the government. Often the committee worked day and night. Its members (including Danton and Marat) ate, slept, and debated in an atmosphere of chaos.

In a desperate attempt to fight the Jacobins, the Girondins accused Marat of plotting to become a dictator. But the end was near for the Girondins. For forty-three days in May and June 1793, riots again swept Paris. The Convention finally threw out the Girondins; twenty-nine Girondin leaders were arrested.

In revenge, Charlotte Corday, a fierce Girondin, decided to kill the man she called "an enemy of humanity"—Marat. On July 13, 1793, she talked her way into Marat's house. Marat was soaking in a bath to relieve the pain of a skin disease. Corday stabbed him to death.

Instantly, Marat became a martyr for the Jacobin cause. Corday was arrested by the Revolutionary Tribunal and sentenced to the guillotine. She told the Tribunal, "I killed one man to save a hundred thousand." Unfortunately, the violence and suffering in France between the fall of 1793 and the summer of 1794 actually increased. This was a period known as the Reign of Terror.

France was still at war with its foreign enemies, but the conflict within France grew worse. The nation's economic situation was as bad as ever. In an attempt to stem France's runaway inflation, the Convention passed the General Maximum Law in September 1793. The law made it illegal to sell goods at more than their price in 1790 plus 30 percent. At the same time, the Maximum allowed wages to increase up to 50 percent of 1790 levels. By fixing wages and prices, the Convention hoped to maintain France's war effort while satisfying calls for higher wages and less inflation.

Robespierre now controlled the Committee of Public Safety. His search for what he thought was justice guided the terrible policies that nearly tore France apart for eleven months. Robespierre was obsessed with the idea of foreign plots, conspiracies, and spies. He believed in Rousseau's ideas of the goodness of the common man. But the cold, intellectual Robespierre was really more interested in his own ideas than in the fate of real people.

The British navy had blockaded France for months, halting trade and bringing the nation to the edge of starvation. In Normandy and Bordeaux, and in cities like Lyons, Toulon, and Marseilles, citizens revolted against the revolutionary cause. But the revolutionary armies slowly battered away at the rebellious cities, capturing them from their royalist defenders. The slaughter was enormous. At Nantes, two thousand people were drowned in a river. In Lyons, over fifteen hundred "rebels" were condemned to death. The guillotine was too slow for this kind of work; groups of condemned people were shot or blown apart by cannon fire.

In Paris, the parade of tumbrils (carts) to the guillotine never seemed to stop. In October 1793, Queen Marie Antoinette was tried and executed. Many Girondin leaders followed the queen, as did Jean-Sylvain Bailly, the former mayor of Paris. Ordinary people went to the guillotine as well, including nuns, priests, journalists, even army officers whose only crime was to lose a battle. An accusation from a jealous but "patriotic" neighbor was often enough to bring imprisonment and death.

This portrait of Marie Antoinette was painted while she was a prisoner. The former queen finally went to the guillotine in October 1793.

Danton, disgusted by the endless executions, left Paris. For a brief moment, it seemed as if a pause in the Terror might be possible. Robespierre himself seemed to listen when Danton called for mercy. But he was determined to establish a "Republic of Virtue" by any means, including terror and death. Robespierre had his old partner in revolution brought to trial in April 1794. Danton defended himself brilliantly before the Tribunal, but opinion was against him. Only three days after the trial began, Danton and five others were executed for corruption, conspiracy, and "hypocrisy." On the way to the guillotine, Danton shouted, "Robespierre will follow me!"

Making the World Anew

As early as 1789, the idea of a new revolutionary calendar appeared in France. For some, the day after the fall of the Bastille—July 15, 1789—was "the second day of liberty, year 1." But it was not until 1793 that France's revolutionary government approved a completely new calendar.

There were several reasons for the change. Supporters of the new calendar wanted to create a new world where all traces of the *ancien régime* would be gone. The old ways of organizing society would be swept away by the new spirit of liberty, equality, and brotherhood.

September 22, 1793, the day the Republic of France was proclaimed, was declared the first day of the first month of Year 1 of the Republic. A committee of poets, artists, and scientists was set up to calculate a new calendar and rename the months, days, and weeks of the year.

The committee divided the year up into twelve months of thirty days each, with three ten-day weeks called *decadi*. The names of the new months were invented by the poet Fabre d'Eglantine to reflect the changing seasons and the rural life that most French people lived. The names of the months were:

Vendemaire	The time of the grape harvest	(Sept./Oct.)
Brumaire	The time of fog	(Oct./Nov.)
Frimaire	The time of frost	(Nov./Dec.)
Nivose	The time of snow	(Dec./Jan.)
Pluviose	The time of rain	(Jan./Feb.)
Ventose	The time of wind	(Feb./ March)
Germinal	The time of sowing	(March/April)
Floreal	The time of flowers	(April/May)
Prairial	The time of meadows	(May/June)
Messidor	The time of the harvest	(June/July)
Thermidor	The time of heat	(July/Aug.)
Fructidor	The time of fruit	(Aug./Sept.)

Five days each year were left over. These were made festival days, called *Sans-Culottides* after the *sans-culottes*. Each celebrated one of the five "revolutionary virtues"—Virtue, Labor, Talent, Heroic Deeds, and Ideas. The Christian holidays, saints' days, and religious feasts that had marked France's calendar for centuries were dropped.

The revolutionary government's antireligious attitude went beyond remaking the calendar. Many priests were forced to give up their vows and marry. The Bishop of Paris had to pledge his belief in "Reason." Statues of saints were torn from cathedrals. In Paris, a "Festival of Reason" was held in the Notre Dame cathedral on November 10, 1793 (20 Brumaire). Speeches and revolutionary songs replaced sermons and hymns. Robespierre organized a "Festival of the Supreme Being" the next year in an attempt to show that the revolution was based on moral principles from a supreme being.

A revolutionary print of the "Republican Calendar."

Many events of the French Revolution are still referred to by their revolutionary calendar names. The date of Robespierre's death, 10 Thermidor, Year II, gave its name to a group of politicians who came to power after the Terror—the Thermidorians. Perhaps the best-remembered date is 20 Brumaire, Year VIII, when Napoléon Bonaparte seized control of the French government.

Old habits die hard, and most people can't accept radical change overnight. The revolutionary calendar lasted only about twelve years, being abolished January 1, 1806.

This revolutionary print celebrates the "Festival of the Supreme Being" organized by Robespierre in June 1794.

By now, the Committee of Public Safety had concentrated all the powers of government in its hands. In June 1794, Robespierre, now the undisputed leader of the government, organized another of the grand festivals that marked the French Revolution.

At the "Festival of the Supreme Being," Robespierre tried to establish a new religion—a religion of the state. There were no priests, and few doctrines other than a belief in the "Supreme Being" and the immortal soul of man. For hours, Robespierre spoke from a platform in the Champ de Mars. The festival celebrated the virtues of wisdom, truth, justice, and freedom. To some, it seemed that Robespierre had begun to think of himself as a god.

Robespierre said, "Virtue without terror is disastrous," and the Terror continued. In six weeks during the summer of 1794, thirteen hundred people were executed in Paris—more than in the entire year before.

The Terror had begun as a means of controlling possible enemies during a national crisis. In the name of "national security," the rule of law and reasonable justice was suspended. But by the end of the summer, French armies were victorious throughout Europe. A foreign invasion seemed unlikely. Why, people asked, should the Terror continue?

But it went on, claiming victims from every group, royalist, bourgeoisie, and *sans-culottes* alike. English writer William Hazlitt described France in those days: "The whole of the country seemed one vast conflagration [fire] of revolt and vengeance. The shrieks of death blended with the yell of the assassin."

Within the revolutionary government, at last, an anti-Robespierre movement began gathering strength. The people were exhausted, and finally several former supporters accused Robespierre of tyranny.

The Convention turned against him. When Robespierre appeared before the Convention, shouts of "Down with the Tyrant!" greeted him. When his voice failed, someone yelled, "The blood of Danton chokes you!"

Robespierre was arrested. During the struggle, he was wounded in the jaw by a pistol shot. (He may have tried to kill himself.) He had no trial. Robespierre went to the guillotine on July 28, 1794, five years and two weeks after the fall of the Bastille.

Wounded in the jaw by his own pistol, Robespierre is arrested in the Convention.

A major phase of the French Revolution ended with Robespierre's death. With the Terror ended, reaction against the original aims of the revolution set in. The moderate bourgeoisie took control of the government, pushing out extremists of the left and right. France was exhausted, but the Revolution was not truly over.

AFTERWORD

The Legacy of the French Revolution

In August 1794, reaction to the revolution was symbolized by gangs of fancily dressed young men. They roamed the streets of Paris, attacking anything that smacked of republicanism. They smashed statues of revolutionary heroes, broke windows at the Jacobin Club, and brawled with Jacobins, *sans-culottes*, and working people.

At the same time, the Convention did away with much of the revolutionary government. The Committee of Public Safety, the Watch Committees, and the Revolutionary Tribunal had their powers reduced, and the Paris Commune was abolished. Prisons were opened. Surviving Girondins, moderates, and royalists were freed. Émigrés began returning to France. Freedom of religion and the press, outlawed during the Terror, were restored.

The bourgeoisie in the government ended wage and price controls that had been introduced in 1793. As a result, inflation and unemployment grew worse. The value of the revolutionary currency, the *assignats*, plunged. In 1794, the price of flour was one hundred times what it had been in 1790.

The winter of 1794 was harsh, and cold weather increased the poor's suffering. While the wealthy and bourgeoisie ate lavishly at restaurants, working people in Paris starved. The price of food continued to rise, until once again people protested in the streets. For some, it seemed that nothing had been changed by the Revolution.

In April 1795, and again in May, mobs stormed the Convention, demanding bread. The National Guard was called out to put down the mobs. This was the last uprising of the left.

In the provinces, émigré landowners returned to claim their lands. Revolutionaries were hunted down and massacred. Peace treaties with Prussia, Spain,

Napoléon Bonaparte wears the robe and laurels of an emperor in this lithograph.

An aristocrat and a republican clash on the streets of Paris in the aftermath of the Terror.

and the Netherlands were signed. Work began on a new constitution.

The new constitution emphasized legal and property rights instead of "natural rights." Universal suffrage (the right to vote) was replaced by a rule that only males over twenty-five who could pay a heavy tax could vote. Only about 30,000 people in all of France could vote.

The authors of the new constitution, eager to guard against both mob rule and tyranny, reorganized the government. Executive power would be held by a Directory of five men. These were to be chosen by the Council of Ancients, one of two legislative bodies. The second was a Council of 500.

Before the five directors could take office in October, however, there was another uprising. This time the rebels were royalists.

On October 5, 25,000 royalists stormed the Convention. The National Guard was called out. Among its officers was a young artillery commander from the island of Corsica named Napoléon Bonaparte. Only 4,000 guardsmen faced the rebels, but Napoléon drew his cannon around the Tuileries Palace and fired. This "whiff of grapeshot" scattered the rebels.

Napoléon had saved the constitution. He also established the army as a major player in France's political conflicts. From then on, whoever won the army's loyalty would be a power to reckon with.

Five years later, Napoléon returned to Paris from foreign wars. Disgusted with the Directory and backed by his loyal army, Napoléon established himself as France's sole ruler. Calling himself "the man of the hour," he declared France needed a leader "made illustrious by glory."

For sixteen years under Napoléon's dictatorship, the ideals of the revolution seemed to be lost. Still, they did not disappear. The spirit behind the motto "Liberty, Equality, Fraternity" could never be erased. France had been forever changed by the Revolution.

Most important of all, the rule of law remained. The days of the ancien régime, with its feudal dues and aristocratic privileges, were gone forever. Talent and work, not just birth, opened the

Napoléon Bonaparte's "whiff of grapeshot" saves the National Convention in October 1795.

doors of opportunity for the French people. Free public education was a legacy of the revolution, as was equal justice for all under the law. The power of the Church, which once rivaled that of royalty, was reduced. A prosperous rural middle class was created when the Church lands were distributed. This stable middle class is still an important force in France.

But the French Revolution left a troublesome legacy as well. The use of violence and terror as a public policy reached a new and terrible height in the 1790s and set a pattern for revolution that continues today. In 1989, France celebrated the Bicentennial of the Fall of the Bastille. The French Revolution as a turning point in history was debated and analyzed. Its legacies—good and bad—remain. The French Revolution did not just transform one country; it changed Europe and much of the world. The end of aristocratic privilege, the rise of universal suffrage, the growth of nationalism, and the idea of the rights of man all come from the French Revolution. Its influence continues today, in France and around the world.

INDEX

Page numbers in *italics* indicate illustrations

SUGGESTED READING

Banfield, Susan. *The Rights of Man, The Reign of Terror: The Story of the French Revolution.* New York: J.B. Lippincott, 1989.

Bernier, Olivier. *Words of Fire, Deeds of Blood: The Monarchy and the French Revolution.* Boston: Little, Brown & Co., 1989.

Cobb, Richard, ed. *Voices of the French Revolution.* Topsfield, Mass.: Salem House Publishers, 1988.

Dowd, David, ed. *The French Revolution.* New York: American Heritage Publishing Co., 1965.

Godechot, Jacques. *The Taking of the Bastille.* New York: Scribner's, 1970.

Hibbert, Christopher. *The Days of the French Revolution.* New York: William Morrow, 1980.

Manceron, Claude. *Blood of the Bastille, 1787-1789: From Calonne's Dismissal to the Uprising of Paris.* New York: Simon & Schuster, 1989.

Rudé, George. *The Crowd in the French Revolution, 1789–1794.* New York: Oxford, 1959.

Schama, Simon. *Citizens: A Chronicle of the French Revolution.* New York: Alfred A. Knopf, 1989.

Picture Credits

The Bettmann Archive: 5, 9, 14.
French Government Tourist Office: 15, 26, 29.
Library of Congress: 18, 28, 43, 44, 51, 55, 57, 58, 60, 61.
Mary Evans Picture Library: 10, 12, 20, 21, 22, 31, 32, 39, 46, 48, 52.
Mary Evans Picture Library/Explorer: 35, 36, 38, 50, 53, 56.

About the Author

Kitty C. Benedict was born in New Jersey and has lived most of her life in New York and New England. After graduating from Smith College, she studied in Italy, where she also taught English on a Fulbright scholarship. An editor in book publishing for fifteen years, she is now a free-lance writer, editor, and book critic.